Heinrich Melchior Muhlenberg
Hero of Faith

By Stephenie M. Hovland
Illustrated by Larry Johnson

CONCORDIA PUBLISHING HOUSE · SAINT LOUIS

Written by Stephenie M. Hovland
Edited by Rodney L. Rathmann
Editorial Assistant: Amanda G. Lansche

Manufactured in East Peoria, IL / 63692 / 160153

Table of Contents

Henry Muhlenberg

He knew he must be strong for his family.

◆ ◆ ◆

chapter one
Coping with Loss

Heinrich could almost smell the fresh, hot bread he knew his mother must be taking out of the oven. He hurried down the street to his eighteenth-century German home, almost running through the door. Mindful of the manners his parents had impressed upon him, he walked in the house quietly and closed the door behind him. The normal noise of a busy household was silenced. And there was no scent of fresh bread. The warmth of the house seemed to be gone. Heinrich knew something was wrong. What had happened?

"Heinrich, is that you?" his mother called from the kitchen. His mother's voice was always strong and confident. Not that day. He could hear weakness and trembling. As he entered the kitchen, he heard someone sobbing. Nobody except children cried in the Muhlenberg house.

Heinrich saw some of the women from church comforting his mother. She held a handkerchief to her face, but Heinrich could see her puffy, glistening eyes ready to spill tears, as they must have been the whole time he was at school.

Mother looked at her friends, and they left the room and closed the door behind them. Heinrich stood in front of his mother, who stayed seated. She looked him in the eyes and said, "Heinrich, your father has passed."

Heinrich looked at her, trying to understand. He knew what *passed* meant, but that word did not belong with his father, a strong, active man. Heinrich looked to the door, expecting his father to walk through and explain his mother's confusion.

She held both of Heinrich's hands and squeezed them. He looked into her eyes again.

"Heinrich, your father is dead," she whispered. She pulled Heinrich close to embrace him. He sniffed and blinked. He knew he must be strong for his family.

Years later, people would say that if it weren't for his father's death, Heinrich might not have developed such a strong character. At the young age of 12, Heinrich wouldn't have been forced to quit school and find a way to help financially support his family. He wouldn't have had to go through his teen years without a father to guide him. He wouldn't have had to work long days in a physical job, reading books and studying God's Word only after all the chores were done. He wouldn't have needed to struggle so hard just to survive.

Although others might have bragged that they did it all themselves, Heinrich knew his strength came from the Lord. His self-reliance was anchored in God. His father would have been proud to see how Heinrich coped, adjusted, and moved forward after his death.

Heinrich knew his strength came from the Lord.

◆ ◆ ◆

chapter two
Determined to Serve

Heinrich Melchior Muhlenberg was born on September 6, 1711, to Claus and Anna Maria Melchior Muhlenberg. After the death of his father, the family finances were often strained. But when he became a young adult, the Muhlenbergs' situation began to slowly improve. Muhlenberg received several scholarships to the University of Goettingen, where he could commit himself to the full-time

study of theology, a subject in which he was very interested.

Early on, Muhlenberg had even practiced his preaching skills in a barn (giving sermons to whichever animals cared to listen). After a few years, his professors urged Muhlenberg to continue preparations to become a pastor. Though he learned the biblical languages of Greek and Hebrew, Muhlenberg also learned other languages (such as English and Dutch) that would be helpful to him when he traveled overseas years later.

Muhlenberg was confirmed in the Lutheran Church. By the time he was twenty-seven years old, Muhlenberg had finished his religious studies by analyzing many of the documents essential to the Lutheran Church, including:

the Apostles' Creed,

the Nicene Creed,

and the Athanasian Creed;

the Augsburg Confession;

the Smalcald Articles,

Luther's Large and Small Catechisms,

and the Formula of Concord.

Of course, he did not consider that to be the end of his theological education. Throughout the rest of his adult life, Muhlenberg eagerly studied the Scriptures, doctrine, and the documents of the Church.

In his first full-time job as an adult, Muhlenberg traveled to Halle, Germany, where he taught at an orphanage. It did not take long for those around him to realize he was humble, smart, and a talented teacher. They gave him more and more responsibility, and his teachers took special notice of his God-given gifts.

"Have you observed the young Muhlenberg?" a balding professor with a gray beard asked his colleague.

"Is he the one recently assigned to work in the orphanage?" asked his friend as they shared their dinner.

The first professor nodded. "Yes. The one who seems to know how to talk to the children about spiritual matters."

"Ah, yes. I have noticed." The second professor nodded in return, then drank from his cup and continued. "There have been others who speak too much, lecturing on and on, as if they are in the seminary with an audience of theologians. But, this young man . . . I have seen that he still gives them solid Scripture and catechism lessons, but he does it in a way the children understand. I daresay some children even ask for him when they have questions."

"Do they really? That is nice. He will make a great teacher. But, I had in mind to see if he could be given a mission call. He is proficient in a few languages already and has shown interest in learning more. I could see him in some far off country such as India. We have the need for a preacher there."

"How is his preaching? Have you read his sermons?" The professor broke off a piece of bread and offered it to his friend.

"Yes. Thank you." The other professor took the piece of bread and placed it next to his cup. "His sermons are very well written. He certainly puts much research and thought into each one. I have also heard him deliver a few. They are adequate for a young man. I can see him improving over time, but he has a solid beginning."

"That is a blessing. I know some young ministers who can teach and counsel but are not so adept at writing a sermon. I recommend they memorize a few of my own sermons and deliver them several times to help develop their skills."

"Ah, no. That will not be necessary with Muhlenberg. I have heard he was writing sermons in his childhood."

Both men smiled and chuckled at the thought, then continued their meal.

While he was in Halle, Muhlenberg came into contact with the Pietist movement. Pietists focused heavily on emotions and behavior. So, for example, they believed that when you had faith, your life outwardly changed. They often didn't allow certain activities, such as dancing and going to the theater. Those things were not considered holy, so a person who truly had faith would not do them. Other Lutherans of that time thought that faith was a work in progress, something that matures and grows—not necessarily an instant change in behavior. They also believed that your emotions were not a measure of your faith. They were critical of the Pietists' simplification of God in our lives, claiming the Pietists' beliefs were based too much on emotions and outward obedience to God's Law instead of focusing on the Gospel and what God does for us.

Some of the people who heard that Muhlenberg was associated with Halle assumed he was a Pietist. Many historians agree that although he was influenced by them, he was not swayed by their beliefs and practices. Muhlenberg did not consider himself a Pietist and often complained when people gave him that label.

Muhlenberg was determined to serve God. He wanted to share God's Word with everyone who would hear him. Soon he would travel long and far to reach people who needed the clear preaching of God's Word, and comfort of assurance of forgiveness in Jesus, and the blessings of the Sacraments.

hero of faith

chapter three
Called to America

After working at the orphanage for a year, Muhlenberg received a call to a church in a German town of two thousand people in Saxony. A *call* is an official assignment to a church that needs a pastor. A pastor does not seek out the church, as in traditional jobs, but the church seeks out the pastor. After praying about the decision, the pastor may either accept or reject the call.

While he was still a pastor at that church, Muhlenberg expected a call to mission work in India. He was also considered for other positions, such as a missionary to Jewish people. But ultimately, God led Muhlenberg to go to the New World to help encourage and organize the Lutherans already there. In 1741, he received a call to go to America and help organize the Lutherans living there. The New World was still a vast and untamed country at this time, full of brave pioneers who traveled there to carve out lives for themselves.

Some Lutherans had tried to start churches in the New World, but they found it difficult because there were very few Lutheran pastors. Sometimes, men pretended to be pastors just so people would pay them to preach or baptize their children. When a church would form and meet in someone's house or barn, the pastor preaching on a given Sunday might have come from a non-Lutheran denomination, such as from Moravian or Reformed Churches. Many problems arose with these methods of securing pastoral care. People became confused by the

differences in theology they heard from these various pastors.

"I cannot deny God's hand in your life, Heinrich." His mother had seen her young child grow into an intelligent man. "I remember hearing noise come from your bedroom one night when you were but thirteen. I was about to scold you for staying up so late and talking to yourself, but I stood by your door and listened. You were reciting passages from Dr. Martin Luther's works. I heard you repeat them, so I knew you were memorizing. So wise. Even back then."

Muhlenberg smiled at his mother, not remembering that night in particular, but thinking back to the many nights when he would come home tired, eat dinner, then retire to his room to study and memorize Scripture and doctrine. He hadn't known that his mother had caught him disobeying bedtime.

"And yet, I cannot help but think you are going to your death." His mother's eyes swelled with tears. "Those savages in the New World, the natives . . . I've heard stories." She wiped a tear away. "I've also heard about the people who emigrate to such a wild country. They are not so noble, you know. Many would rather not hear of God or have a pastor insist on them going to church."

"I know, Mother." Muhlenberg held her hand and patted it, reassuring her gently. "I know that this is an amazing mission in a faraway place, but remember that my primary purpose is to help the good Lutherans. Think of the German people living there who now find themselves with no pastor. They struggle to build churches and keep the doors open. They have been begging for someone to come and help them for years now. I cannot deny—"

"Yes, yes. . . . Of course." She nodded. "God has given you the gifts for such a job. I pray you think of your lonely mother and send me many letters. It is your duty to honor me, you know. Write every week. Tell me you are still alive."

Muhlenberg chuckled. "Oh, Mother. I will survive. You need not worry. I promise to write as often as I am able. The call is only for three short years. If they still deem me fit for the position, we will talk after that. But, I may very possibly be back in this room talking to you in just a few years."

He stood up and kissed his mother on the forehead, then hugged her and left for London, where he would make final preparations before going overseas.

That was the last time he and his mother would see each other in this life.

On June 13, 1742, Muhlenberg boarded a ship headed to Georgia in America. He planned to visit many southern churches before traveling north to Pennsylvania, where most of his work would take place.

hero of faith

chapter four

A Rough Voyage

For 102 days, Muhlenberg endured a nightmare of a journey. Between the threat of pirate attacks, constant severe sickness, and life with the interesting people on board (not to mention the rats!), he might have questioned whether he should have taken the voyage at all. But, through it all, Muhlenberg remained faithful and steadfast in the service of his God and Savior. When he heard sailors or fellow passengers using God's name in vain or taking part in other sinful activities, he fearlessly and directly talked with them about it.

When they acknowledged and repented of their sins, he comforted and encouraged them with the Good News of Jesus and the forgiveness He earned long before on the cross.

Muhlenberg wrote in his diary:

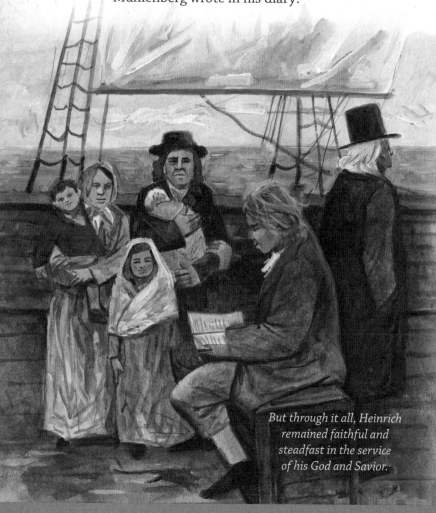

But through it all, Heinrich remained faithful and steadfast in the service of his God and Savior.

I thank God that I am traveling with at least one family with whom I may converse. They are formerly from Salzburg and, thus, speak in my native tongue. Nevertheless, I do get to practice the English language, which may come in handy in the New World. Although I do not understand all English words, I am quite sure that many uttered in drunkenness aboard this ship I do not wish to know!

Some days, I am not sure this vessel is seaworthy. In the event of an attack, which I pray daily does not happen, we have at least ten iron cannons and a variety of weapons. I am told that I may have to defend the ship as a soldier if we are attacked. Apparently, they have not noticed my wretched condition. When I am not nauseated from the swaying of this ship, I am feverish with who knows what disease. I can only imagine, with all the rats scurrying about and getting into our limited water supply. I will welcome dry land and any difficulties that God may set before me in the new land, if only I can live to see it!

Muhlenberg set foot on American soil for the first time on September 23, 1742, in Charleston, South Carolina. After spending some time visiting southern churches, he was anxious to get up north before Christmas. The only way he could get there in a speedy manner was to take a sloop, a small ship with sails. Once again, he fell ill. At one point, the sloop took on so much water that Muhlenberg said anything would have been more pleasant than that ride. But, even as his stomach churned, Muhlenberg preached Sunday sermons in both German and English for the people on board, sometimes speaking from his bed when he was too weak to sit up.

After he arrived in Pennsylvania, he stayed off boats as much as possible!

hero of faith

chapter five

Problems and Opportunities

Muhlenberg soon found plenty of work. There were so many needy people. According to the papers with his official call, he was supposed to minister primarily to three Lutheran congregations: New Hanover, Philadelphia, and Providence. That wasn't as easy as it might seem. Often, the travel itself was hazardous, especially during the winter when he fought against ice and bitter cold. Muhlenberg often found himself wet and shivering, sometimes up to his horse's belly in snow. He also often became sick, although he had been a healthy person when he left Europe.

As if the physical obstacles weren't enough, he soon found himself heavily involved in many conflicts. Some preachers who had been ministering to the Lutherans didn't want Muhlenberg to come. Most of those who had problems with him had problems of their own. Some had never been to a seminary to take theology courses, so they weren't officially pastors. Others lived in drunkenness and committed sexual immorality. Some weren't Lutheran, yet wanted to preach in the Lutheran churches. Muhlenberg came to remedy the problems caused by these situations.

As he traveled to churches and homes, he heard of people's troubles. Some simply abandoned their Lutheran beliefs and began attending other churches. One man

explained, "Since we didn't have a Lutheran pastor here, and we thought nobody would come, we decided not to be Lutheran any more. There's a Moravian church near our home, so that's where we go."

An older man who had been one of the early settlers complained, "When the Reformed preacher would come, he stirred up arguments about the Sacraments in our church. After many discussions, our congregation split into different groups that couldn't get along. Some even fought over who should keep our church building. We spent years raising money and building that church. None of us can let it go, but we can't worship together anymore."

"We didn't know what to do," said a woman as she paused in hanging clothing on the clothesline. "We have no Lutheran pastor and wouldn't think of going to a different church. So, we don't go to church. Unfortunately, we have been so busy just trying to get by that we haven't brought up our children with Luther's Catechism. They've never even gone to church."

"What are you going to do when your child must be baptized and you need Communion? We're good Lutherans. We know we need our Sacraments. We paid the traveling pastors who charge for such services. Rumor is, though, that they may not be pastors at all, and that they spend all the money getting drunk. But what are we supposed to do?" a young father asked as he threw up his hands in frustration.

So Muhlenberg faced many challenges as he visited German Lutherans in America. Little by little, he dealt with problems by teaching the catechism to children and adults, offering Baptism and Communion without charging money, helping mediate disputes, and hosting as many church services as possible all over the countryside.

◆ ◆ ◆

chapter six
God Sends Helpers

Muhlenberg labored over the three churches, trying to meet their needs. He saw the churches at Philadelphia and Providence start building comfortable houses of worship instead of meeting in people's homes and barns, while the New Hanover church worked to build a school. Building permanent structures like these was very encouraging for everyone involved, despite the concerns about money. Muhlenberg often asked for financial help from his supporters in Europe.

As he worked with more and more Lutherans, word spread that a good Lutheran pastor was in the land. Muhlenberg fulfilled as many requests for his services as he could, but he was soon begging his superiors to send more help. He was not lazy or even wanting to take a break. His compassion for so many people who desperately wanted his presence was too much for one man. He knew he could only do so much.

On January 26, 1745, Muhlenberg had the pleasure of welcoming three young men to Philadelphia. Peter Brunnholz, John Kurtz, and John Schaum were missionaries who came to work under Muhlenberg.

He would decide where and how they were going to serve the area.

It seems as though the timing of these new workers could not have been better. Shortly after they arrived, Muhlenberg found time to get married.

I did find a worthy woman, who I married on April 22, 1745.
Miss Anna Mary Weiser, daughter of Conrad Weiser, became my wife.

Muhlenberg says in his diary:

I had planned to remain unmarried my whole life,
to dedicate every hour to the ministry and not get distracted
by the commitments of being a husband and father.
But, everywhere I went, people had a daughter or neighbor
who would make a great wife. Or so I was told.
I could never escape the matchmaking of these people,
whether I was in the city or the country.
It never mattered and never stopped.

As it turns out, I found myself needing help that would
best be served by a wife. When sick or entertaining a visitor,
it was difficult to manage by myself. If I needed to meet
with female parishioners, that was also a problem.
I did not need rumors starting! So, eventually, I decided
I might want a wife to share in the ministry. Maybe
she could help with my various responsibilities and burdens.

So, I searched for a good Christian woman. She had to
be young, willing to support me in the Lord's work, and
have plenty of energy. My congregations witnessed my
search and had plenty to gossip about. I did find a worthy
woman whom I married on April 22, 1745. Miss Anna
Mary Weiser, daughter of Conrad Weiser, became my wife.

♦ ♦ ♦

chapter seven
Order and Organization

Muhlenberg and his co-workers in the faith had many, many stories to tell. Although they found much encouragement from the Lutherans who had waited for years for guidance, they often found even more opposition. People told false stories about them and confronted them with arguments against Lutheran theology. Discouragement abounded. But, Muhlenberg now had the companionship, help, and support of his wife, his first child, and the three men who came from Germany. Before, he had shouldered these responsibilities by himself. Now, he didn't have to face the challenges alone.

Another missionary, J. F. Handschuh, was sent from Germany in the spring of 1748. He arrived during a turning point in the history of the American Lutheran Church. Even though the pastors still felt discouraged, they gained hope from promising signs of unity and strength among fellow Lutherans in America.

In August of 1748, a group of Lutheran pastors met with Muhlenberg and agreed on a common liturgy, called the Lutheran Orders of Service; it was familiar to the men from when they had lived in Germany. A common, unified liturgy was an important step for the group because it helped others understand more about Lutherans and reinforced Lutheran theology during each service. This group wanted their churches to be identifiable as Lutheran through their worship services as well as through their theology. Also, if people traveled and stopped in at a Lutheran church that was using the liturgy, they would feel comfortable and welcome since they would be familiar with the order of service.

Later that year, in August, about seventy churches were represented at the first meeting of the first Lutheran synod in America. The churches sent pastors and lay representatives (leaders in the church who were not pastors) who together formed this synod, a group of churches that agreed on theology and other church matters. Pastors wanted this synod to help strengthen the Lutheran Church in the New World so that, with the help of one another, Lutherans would be better able to face opposition and could support and encourage one another in the faith.

At that first momentous meeting, Muhlenberg
served as chairman, and Pastor Handschuh was appointed
as the secretary. Muhlenberg gave a speech about the
importance of forming the synod, explaining that working together would strengthen individual churches so
they would not break under the pressure of opposition.
United, the synod could build a firm foundation for future
generations. Plus, as an organized church, they could
better work with churches and church leaders in Europe.

About seventy churches were represented at the first meeting of the first Lutheran synod in America.

General business was discussed, such as how the pastors were doing at their churches, the new liturgy, the parochial schools, and pastors who were not invited to attend because they were not united with the group (some who were not ordained or refused to use the liturgy, for example). The meeting closed with a hymn and an agreement to meet in Lancaster in 1749. Muhlenberg, who had served the American Lutherans for six years already, now served as the first president of the synod (1760 to 1771).

I feel that faith has
traveled from my head
to my heart . . .

◆ ◆ ◆

chapter eight
Strengthening the Synod

Since Muhlenberg's arrival, the three Pennsylvanian churches had gained much stability and strength. The Lutherans who lived in New York requested that he come for a time and try to do the same for them, so he decided to leave his churches and family behind for sixth months to see if he could organize and strengthen those living farther north as well. It was not easy for him to leave his family behind. Though his wife, Anna Mary, and his children understood the importance of his work, they always missed him greatly when it took him so far from home.

As a child, Muhlenberg had learned languages easier than other students. He had found this talent useful in communicating with others in America. While in New York, Muhlenberg did something that others found amazing— he preached in three languages every Sunday. Preaching in Dutch, German, and English allowed him to minister better to diverse groups, including immigrants who still spoke their native languages.

Working with several languages made sermon preparation much more difficult, but he was determined to serve the people and God in the best way possible!

At one New York parish, Muhlenberg visited several times with a man in his twenties or thirties.

"Herr Muhlenberg?" The young man approached the pastor after a Sunday afternoon service.

"Yes?"

"I know we have met a few times to discuss salvation and some things I have been confused about. I was wondering if we might meet again this evening? Perhaps over dinner?"

"Certainly. What would you like to discuss this time?" Muhlenberg awaited the response as the young man looked down at his feet. He paused, then looked into the pastor's eyes with a smile and reddened cheeks.

"I . . . I have been feeling very different lately." He paused, looked down, then began again. "I heard Bible stories as a child, memorized prayers and hymns. I love to sing. But . . . " He looked up and smiled again. "After a sermon, when you choose a hymn for us to study, right there in church . . .

I cannot believe what I hear. Wait. Yes, I can! I am amazed at those hymns I have sung from memory since I was a child. They have such deep meaning. They have brought me closer to Jesus Christ. You have brought me closer. I feel that faith has traveled from my head to my heart . . ."

"Ah," replied Muhlenberg with a knowing smile. "I could talk about that all night long. I will see you at dinner time."

God indeed works in wonderful ways, thought Muhlenberg. *And he works in the lives of His servants.*

Wherever he went, Muhlenberg tried to strengthen the churches in the Lutheran doctrine and the people in their spiritual journeys. He also worked to recover the reputation of Lutheran pastors; imposters had made them look bad in the past. Even some of the trained Lutheran preachers had very public sinful problems of which they failed to repent. Some got drunk or were easily angered. Others spent too much money or focused on themselves. Muhlenberg continued to work on enlarging the synod to include more congregations, strengthening their pastors in God's Word so these problems would be less and less common among Lutherans. As Lutheran pastors supported and encouraged one another, they became stronger, more faithful servants of God and His Church.

As president of the synod, uniting and strengthening the churches was no longer just a desire of his, but it was his job, his calling. As a pastor, he needed to be concerned primarily with the churches he served as pastor. But as the synod's president, he tried to visit as many places as possible to continue to mediate disputes and to strengthen and unify the Lutheran churches.

hero of faith

chapter nine
Growing Pains

In April 1763, the Muhlenberg family said farewell to the three eldest boys, Peter (age 16), Frederick (age 13), and Henry (age 9), who were sent to Germany to study at Halle. Pastor and Mrs. Muhlenberg wanted their sons to have a solid, disciplined religious education such as was available to Muhlenberg as a young man. So, they sent them on a ship to London, then on to Germany. A judge who was also traveling to Europe kept the boys company and made sure they arrived safely.

Although Muhlenberg and his wife had eight more children at home, they were not eager to see the boys go. They would miss them greatly, but they believed a good education was essential to their boys' futures—and they were not wrong! All three boys grew up to play important roles in the Lutheran Church and in the early history of the United States.

Back in the New World, Muhlenberg shared with his fellow Lutherans his dreams of building an institution that would house orphans, train men to become pastors, and care for old, sick pastors who had no family nearby to help them. It was quite a large project to consider, seeing as most of the Lutherans in the New World at that time had their hands full supporting their own families and their local pastors! Eventually, Muhlenberg's dreams became reality, but it was not during his lifetime. Since Muhlenberg's time, however, Lutherans have become known for their establishment of charitable and educational institutions, including colleges, universities, seminaries, orphanages, and homes for the elderly and persons with special needs.

In the fall of 1763, Muhlenberg, then age 52, experienced the growing pains of the Lutheran Church in America. He also saw first-hand the birth of the United States of America. When he had moved to America years earlier, his mother had imagined his death at the hands of the "native savages." Muhlenberg's father-in-law, Conrad Weiser, was well-known for his knowledge of the languages and customs of the Native Americans and for his good relationships with them. He helped Muhlenberg learn more about the Native Americans with whom he worked. Over the years, Muhlenberg noticed changes in their behaviors. Concern over relationships between Europeans and Native Americans became especially intense when both the French and English sought them as allies in the conflict that became known as the French and Indian War (1754-1763). Fears and rumors of attacks were especially troubling to Muhlenberg and his family and parishioners during this formative period in the history of America.

Diary entry, October 22, 1763:

Today there was rumor in the city that the Six Nations Indians, who have been loyal to us, have declared war on the English living here. They say all natives in America have united to destroy all white people under the power of the English, which includes even those of us who are from Germany, since this is considered an English territory. Within three months they will come to Philadelphia to begin their conquest.

Now, I figure most rumors are greatly exaggerated, if not completely false, but today a reputable messenger told us the news of a great massacre of our settlers near Wyoming Valley. The native people say they had the backing of the French fleet to carry out this massacre and will have it for many more to come.

Serving as a pastor in early American history provided plenty of adventures, including many battles with nature itself. On October 30, 1763, Pastor Muhlenberg wrote the following:

This morning, during the worship service in Germantown,
we were praying. In the middle of the Third Petition
of the Lord's Prayer, we heard a rumbling like that
of several coaches rolling past the church windows.
Then, I felt the floor tremble and shake. I looked
over to the pulpit as I tried to stay standing. The pulpit
swayed to and fro, threatening to crash to floor.
I stopped praying when I finally realized it was
an earthquake. I looked out at the congregation to see
people's faces turn pale and contort in fear,
as some began to cry or scream.
I could see that a stampede of people all trying to get
outside would surely end in injury or even death,
so I yelled to them to be calm, sit still, and trust
that they were all in God's hands. I reminded them
that we were still in prayer. I began the Lord's Prayer
again as they sat down. We finished with our shaky voices,
then continued with a hymn, our voices choking up a bit. We
managed to finish the service with no injury,
but very shaken spirits.

In the middle of the Third Petition of the Lord's Prayer, we heard a rumbling like that of several coaches rolling past the church window.

Muhlenberg took the earthquake as a sign of God's warning. He encouraged his members to go to their homes and spend the evening in prayer and reflection. For some, this experience ushered in a time of spiritual awakening. They became convicted of their sins and moved to sincere repentance. Many of his congregation members said they felt a stronger faith in God after that event.

Muhlenberg served his Lord during a time of turbulence and rapid change. Soon, the thirteen colonies would engage in a war with England, contending for their right to form a free and independent nation. But, this was also a time of great personal satisfaction and blessing for Muhlenberg and his family. Remember the three boys Muhlenberg and his wife had sent off to receive an education in Europe?

All three returned and became prominent leaders in the early history of the United States.

Henry Muhlenberg, the youngest of the three, served as a Lutheran pastor in the city of Philadelphia at the time of the Revolutionary War. When the British entered Philadelphia in 1777, Henry arrived

on his parents' doorstep late one night, completely unrecognizable. He had escaped from the
British by disguising himself as an Indian!

Frederick Muhlenberg also entered the
ministry. He was a Lutheran pastor in New York
City at the beginning of the Revolutionary War,
but later entered politics. He became the first
Speaker of the House of Representatives.

Peter Muhlenberg was serving as a pastor
in Virginia when he became a close friend of
George Washington. Peter was also a member
of the Virginia House of Burgesses. Here, he
heard Patrick Henry make his famous speech
that ended with the words "Give me liberty or
give me death!"

Soon after, Peter was leading worship in
his congregation. Peter conducted the service
in good order, but under his clerical robe he
wore his officer's uniform. At the end of the
service, Peter pulled off his robes and announced,

"There is a time for all things, a time to preach and a time to pray, but there is also a time to fight, and that time has now come!" Some three hundred of his parishioners followed him to the battlefield.

In 1783, Peter became a major general in the United States Army and served valiantly at the battle of Yorktown. After the war, he served the young nation in a number of ways, including as a United States senator from Pennsylvania.

hero of
faith

◆ ◆ ◆

chapter ten

An Active Retirement

For thirty-two years, Muhlenberg served the Lutheran immigrants in the New World. From the physical hardships of the landscape, the weather, and personal sickness to the difficulties of dealing with opposition in theology and personality, he persevered.

Eventually, old age started to affect Muhlenberg. He faced more and more health problems, including a lack of energy and poor hearing. He retired from his Philadelphia congregation about the same time that Philadelphia became very active with political events. Muhlenberg preferred the peacefulness of the countryside, so he moved to New Hanover.

After traveling so much and maintaining the long hours of a very active pastor and synodical president, Muhlenberg wasn't happy to just sit at home. He helped out at the church in New Hanover and worked from home on projects that didn't require as much physical effort.

One such project was a Lutheran hymnbook, which the synod felt would further unite the Lutheran congregations. They asked Muhlenberg to collect and choose hymns fitting for their book. He was very thoughtful about which hymns to include. They had to build up the Church and individuals by including solid biblical verses. He chose many old German hymns, but also included some newer ones—so long as they had strong theology. The Lutheran hymnbook was published in 1786.

Another book the synod published in 1786 was the Liturgy, which complemented the hymnbook

The Lutheran hymnbook was published in 1786.

very well. It was Muhlenberg's desire that all Lutheran churches in the synod use both books in their services as an act of unity.

Thankfully, Muhlenberg was able to finish those two important worship resources before his death in 1787. He could never have been called lazy in his service to the Church. Even in his final days, he kept his diary and cared for the local Lutherans. The following are but a few entries from Muhlenberg's diary. These accounts tell us of some of his activities during this period in his life.

July 5, 1787—A carpenter and mason arrived today to work on the house. Inside, a painter is working. I wish I could fix it up, but my swollen legs keep me in a chair much of the time. I feel like a fever is coming on, similar to the one I had about a year ago. I rested a lot today.

July 20, 1787—I took a journey to New Hanover. Though not far, I now suffer more dizziness and pain in my arms and legs because of that trip.

July 23, 1787—Still feeling dizzy from that trip. I am swelling more and more. So ill feeling, I can't read or write much today.

August 15, 1787—Still dizzy and quite swollen, but able to study Scriptures and talk with visitors today.

September 23, 1787—Prayed with widow who has similar health complaints. We laugh at our bodies' aging habits and pray that God delivers us from them soon.

September 29, 1787—Baptized Anna, daughter of John and Hanna Frey. She was fifteen months old.

Early Sunday morning, October 7, 1787, about a week after the baptism of baby Anna, Heinrich Melchior Muhlenberg died in Trappe, Pennsylvania. He was buried near the church on October 10.

Heinrich Melchior Muhlenberg

It should be noted that Heinrich is sometimes referred to as Henry instead of Heinrich. Some have suggested that he changed his name to Henry to be more appealing to different nationalities; Heinrich is a very German name.

Whether that is true or not, he did reach out to many different people. And yet, he was careful to never become too worldly. He came to the New World to share God's Word with the people there, not to build up earthly wealth or take up the sinful habits of many residents of his new land.

Though he was humble, Muhlenberg acquired a good reputation for his life of faithful service as a pastor and leader. He didn't work to be recognized. He did not write letters and keep diaries to be honored in the future, but he is honored just the same. We recognize that he played an important part in helping Lutheranism take hold and grow in early America.

hero of faith

Timeline of Events

during Heinrich Melchior Muhlenberg's Life

1711 Heinrich Melchior Muhlenberg is born (September 6)

1723 Muhlenberg's father died

1724 Gabriel Fahrenheit invents the first mercury thermometer

1728 Vitus Bering explores the strait that now bears his name

1732 Benjamin Franklin begins publishing *Poor Richard's Almanac*

1738–1741 Muhlenberg works at Halle orphanage

1742 Muhlenberg leaves London to go to America (June 13); Handel's *Messiah* is performed for the first time

1742 Muhlenberg arrives in America (September 23)

1745 Brunnholz, Kurtz, and Schaum arrive in America (January 26)

1745 Muhlenberg marries Anna Mary Weiser (April 22)

1748 Lutheran churches agree to common liturgy (April 28); *Now I Lay Me Down to Sleep* appears in New England Primer

1748 The first Lutheran synod in America is formed (August 14)

1749 17-year-old George Washington becomes a land surveyor

1750 Johann Sebastian Bach dies

1752 Ben Franklin performs his famous experiment with the kite in the lightning storm

1754 French and Indian War begins

1763 French and Indian War ends

1773 Boston Tea Party

1775 Revolutionary War begins

1776 Declaration of Independence

1778 Captain Cook lands on Hawaiian Islands

1781 Spanish found Los Angeles

1783 Treaty of Paris ends Revolutionary War

1787 Heinrich Melchior Muhlenberg dies (October 7); United States Constitution written